COLONIAL AMERICAN
★ ★ ★ CRAFTS ★ ★ ★
The Village

COLONIAL AMERICAN
★ ★ ★ CRAFTS ★ ★ ★
The Village

By Judith Hoffman Corwin

FRANKLIN WATTS
New York/London/Toronto/Sydney/1989

For Virginia Dare,
the first child born of settlers
in this brave new land
(August 18, 1587),
and all the others that followed,
especially, my son, Oliver Jamie.

Library of Congress Cataloging-in-Publication Data

Corwin, Judith Hoffman.
    Colonial American crafts : the village / by Judith Hoffman Corwin.
        p.   cm.
    Includes index.
    Summary: Includes recipes and instructions for other projects
relating to village life in colonial America.
    ISBN 0-531-10715-9
    1. Handicraft—United States—Juvenile literature.   2. Cookery,
American—Juvenile literature.   3. United States—Social life and
customs—Colonial period, ca. 1600–1772—Juvenile literature.
[1. Handicraft.   2. Cookery, American.   3. United States—Social
life and customs—Colonial period, ca. 1600–1775.]   I. Title.
TT23.C663   1989
745.5—dc20   89-8966 CIP AC

Contents

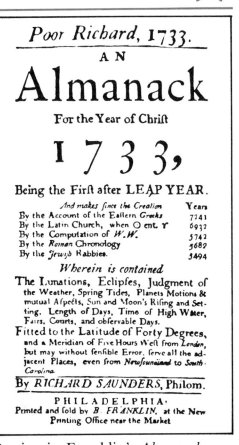

Benjamin Franklin's *Almanack*

"Fractur" writing, or hand decorated picture

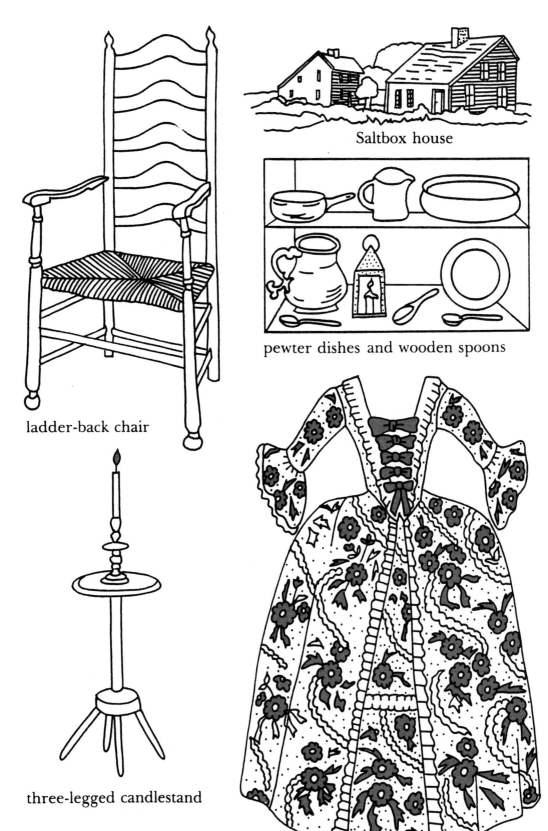

ladder-back chair

Saltbox house

pewter dishes and wooden spoons

three-legged candlestand

1700s American dress

About This Book ★

This book deals with the colonial period in America, from about 1607 to 1776, just before the signing of the Declaration of Independence. During this time, the colonists were settling into their new environment and were establishing a new life for themselves. We will discover that everyday things—houses, furniture, clothes, tools, food, toys, dishes, candlesticks, and even nails—can all express the character of the time in which the colonists lived.

The first European immigrants to the vast untamed coast of America came to Plymouth, Massachusetts; to New Netherland (which is now New York state); to the Middle Colonies such as New Jersey, Pennsylvania, Maryland, and Delaware; to North and South Carolina; and to Virginia. These first settlers braved the challenge of survival in an unknown land thousands of miles from familiar surroundings, family, and friends. They came for many different reasons, such as the possibility of a brand-new way of life that offered religious freedom, a chance to own their own land, or the promise of a better future.

The colonists came from many countries—England, France, Holland, Germany, and Spain. They brought with them their different customs and skills. There was an exchange of cultures between these settlers and the first Americans—the Indians. The combining of these cultures and the cleverness of using the materials that were found in the "New World" resulted in a new and exciting way of life.

The living conditions were simpler then, and the general knowledge of the first settlers was less extensive than it is today. Daily life was similar to what it would be like for us on a camping trip. Life depended on the weather and on the seasons. The early settlers had only the bare necessities of life.

The colonists found it very hard work to survive in this strange, new land. If they were lucky enough to live through the rough sea voyage, many died during their first years here. They relied on the friendly Indians for help in learning how to grow new foods like corn, cranberries, pumpkins, and squash and where to hunt and fish. The settlers built homes for themselves and their families. At first, some dug caves in the hills or built tipis like the ones the Indians lived in. Other early structures were made from logs with sailcloth stretched over them and raised stockades.

Eventually, the people were able to build and develop towns with wood frame, stone, and brick houses; a mill; a blacksmith's shop; taverns; a schoolhouse; a bakery; a print shop; a lacemakers' shop; a music shop; a general store; a church; a meetinghouse; and even a wigmaker's shop. By the year 1733, there were thirteen colonies. The men and women had to know how to plant and harvest crops, tend to livestock, cook and preserve their own food, make candles, weave cloth, make their own clothes, shear sheep, cure ills, forecast weather, and even embroider and sew patchwork quilts. Children worked hard alongside their parents in order for their family to survive and eventually prosper.

When America was young, almost everything people needed was handmade. The colonists took great pride in the things that they made for everyday use. These everyday items were functional, and many were beautifully crafted. Early American colonists gave us a heritage rich in charming customs and wonderful arts and crafts. We can learn from what they were able to develop and make use of.

Honesty, hard work, a sensible nature, and the ability to work together to solve their problems enabled the colonists to survive in a hostile environment. Try to imagine what life was like in the 1600s and 1700s in this young country. Open, unexplored, bountiful land; natural resources beyond belief; and natural beauty. No car, bus, or airplane noise. All food was grown on your land or nearby or caught in the forest.

There was no fast food, and no radio, television, or home computers. There was no electricity or gas for lighting, warmth, or cooking. Your food was cooked on the open hearth in the middle of the kitchen. Your clothes were made at home by someone in your family, fashioned out of linen or wool made on your farm. You had only a few changes of clothes, and probably only one pair of shoes. Bicycles, skateboards, video games, chocolate bars, and ice cream would not be in your world.

One of the values of history is that it enables us to better understand both the people of other times and ourselves. A peek into the world of eighteenth-century America, when the nation was just beginning, is an exciting look at a trying time, but also a time of opportunity for new beginnings and a chance to be free.

There are three books in the "Colonial American Crafts" series—*The Home*, *The Village*, and *The School*. All three have participation projects that use crafts to provide insights into the lives of colonial people.

spinning wheel

grandfather clock

bark-roof dugout house

The Village

The history of the American people starts with the colonists' arrival on these shores, their struggle for survival in this vast wilderness full of natural beauty and wonder about to begin.

Upon arrival, shelter was a first necessity. Captain John Smith said this about the first shipload of settlers:

> Now falleth every man to work, the
> council contrive the fort, the rest
> cut down trees to make place to pitch
> their tents, some provide clapboards
> to relade the ships, some make gardens . . .

The first settlers used the crudest methods of building, with whatever material was at hand. The structures were similar to the shelters of the Indians. Such shelters, whether tents or tipis, were, of course, intended to last only long enough for the colonists to build something more permanent. The goal was to provide shelter in a relatively short amount of time for all the inhabitants of the colony.

Colonial American homes were very simple. They were usually built of wood, brick, or stone. Rough logs were hewn into square timbers to make the frame for a wooden house. At first, the roofs were thatched or covered with bark. Eventually, wooden shingles were used to replace the thatched roofs. These houses had one large room with a sleeping loft. As the family grew, other smaller rooms would be added to the sides of the house. There was a dirt floor, which became smooth and hard after months of wear. On holidays, designs were scratched into the floor to decorate it. Holly designs would be etched in front of the hearth on Christmas, and on birthdays, greetings would be made.

The houses didn't have glass windows because it was too expensive and glass was hard to obtain. Instead, the people used oiled paper or rows of bottles that were mortared into the wall openings to let the light of day into their homes.

The German and Dutch colonists preferred to build their homes out of brick and stone, like the ones that were built in their homeland. In the South, the homes were more elaborate and there were large estates.

As ordinary people didn't have the means to erect houses that were as well built as those constructed by wealthier people, their houses were not so durable. As generations pass, there has been a steady disappearance of these houses, whereas the finer homes remain as a reminder of the people who once inhabited them. A person who prospers is likely to tear down an earlier house and build a better one in its place. Therefore, it is not surprising that few of the earliest houses built in America—whether in Virginia, Pennsylvania, Massachusetts, or Connecticut—remain. For the most part, we know little of what they looked like. In many cases, a few lines of description or a passing reference in a text is all we have.

The earliest house in the English colonies still standing was built in 1651, twenty years after the settlement of the Massachusetts Bay Colony and thirty years after the Pilgrims landed at Plymouth. It is called the Scotch or Boardman House at Saugus in Massachusetts. It was built to receive Scotch prisoners captured by Oliver Cromwell in 1650.

In various parts of the country, distinct types of houses developed, types suited to the climate and to the occupations and social life of the people in that region.

The colonists grouped their homes and farms together to form small communities or villages. This provided protection and security, and they were able to trade goods with each other and help neighbors. Villages began growing around river and sea ports where supplies were brought in by ships from Europe. Flour mills and sawmills that used the water-powered grinders and saws made work easier. The mills were the center of these early villages.

18th century New England houses

As mentioned before, almost everything that the family needed was produced at home, and supplies, goods, and services were traded among the colonists in the village. The village provided a central place for business and a place to make social contact with friends and neighbors.

A typical village had a cluster of buildings that included a church, with a steeple that was the highest point in the village, a meetinghouse, a schoolhouse, a flour mill, a sawmill, a blacksmith's shop, a general store, a post office, a printer's shop, and an inn or tavern where travelers could stay while visiting the town. Taverns served meals and had rooms upstairs for the weary traveler. Townspeople could also socialize in the tavern, have some beer or ale, play a game of pool, exchange local gossip, and just relax. Traveling salesmen who carried their wares from village to village or teachers who were hired during the few months that school was in session stayed at the inn or tavern.

The first settlers built their homes around a community pasture. Then the church and businesses were built along the meadow's edge, and other homes were added behind the original row of houses. Footpaths and bridle paths for horses and horse-drawn carriages were left in between. These eventually became the village streets. Later on, they were paved with broad stones and lanterns provided light. As more houses were built and new streets were formed, the grassy pasture in the center of town became a park known as the village green.

A town crier announced any news to the townspeople. He walked through the village holding a long pole with a bell attached. The ringing of the bell attracted the attention of the villagers, and they surrounded the crier as he told the news of the day: the arrival of a new person, any new laws that had been passed in the town council, the arrival of new supplies available at the general store, and the docking or departing of a ship.

As you have seen, the colonial period was an exciting time. The projects that follow will help to bring the colonial village alive. You will be able to share some of the experiences of those days.

16

Village Mural

★

This charming mural has many of the different types of buildings that a colonial village had—houses, a mill, a blacksmith's shop, a tavern, a schoolhouse, a bakery, a general store, a church, and a meetinghouse. The shops have little signs on them and there is even a flagpole with "Old Glory" on it. Trees, animals, and flowers can also be added. Check the illustration for ideas and try some of your own. You can arrange the buildings as you like.

Here's what is needed:

2 yards of muslin, or half of a clean twin-size sheet, pencil
colored felt-tip markers, tape
large sheet of brown wrapping paper

Here's how to do it:

1. You will need a large, clean working surface, like the floor, where you can tape down your muslin. First prepare your work surface by placing a sheet of brown wrapping paper under your muslin. Move the paper as you work so that the markers don't go through the muslin. The tape will help to hold the muslin in place while you are drawing. Place a piece of tape on each of the corners and on the top and bottom of the muslin.

2. Choose which designs you are going to make and then sketch them onto the muslin with a pencil. You might want to make a rough sketch on a piece of scrap paper first to plan out your village. After you have decided what your village is going to look like, begin to draw it onto the muslin with a pencil.

3. With a black marker, go over the pencil lines of your mural. Then color in the village. Add details like grass, flowers, insects, and so on, anything that you like. Draw a border around the whole mural, as shown, and sign it. This makes a nice family or classroom project.

house

house

mill

"Old Glory"

blacksmith shop

tavern

LION INN

19

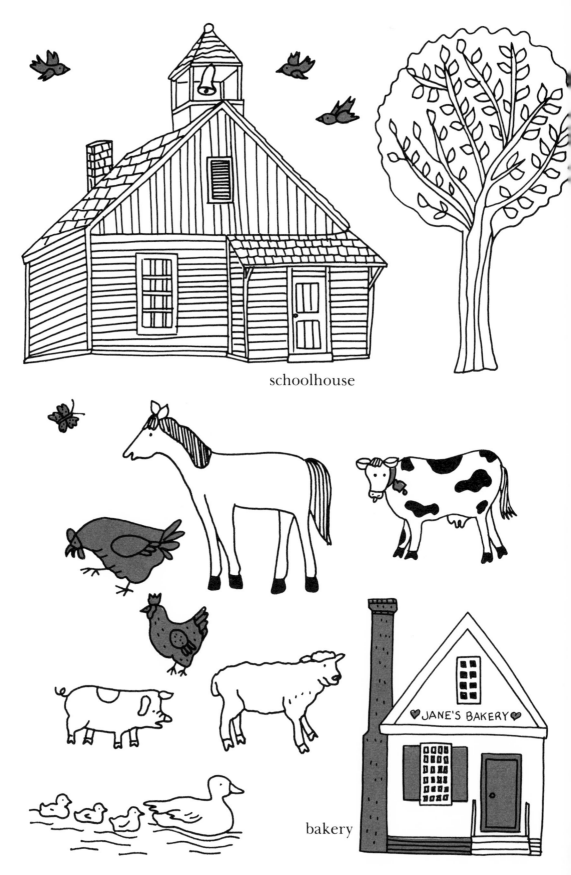

schoolhouse

bakery

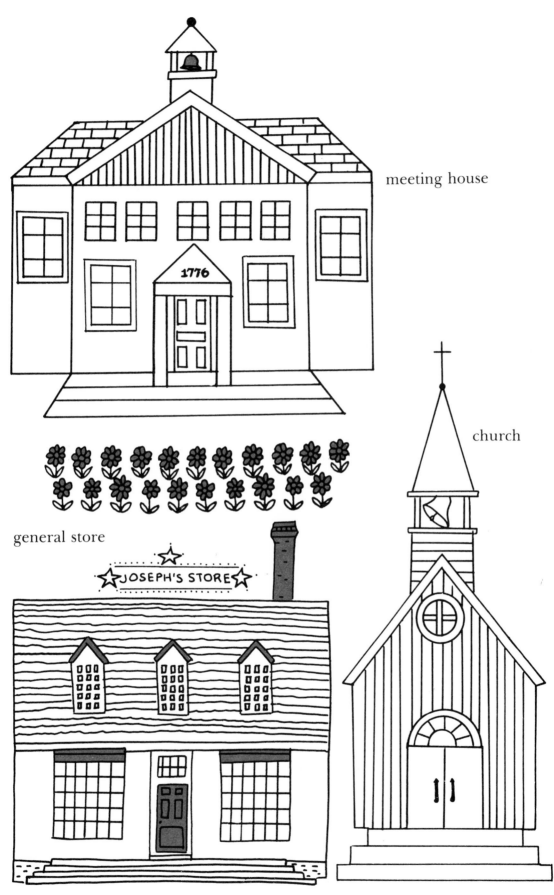

meeting house

church

general store

JOSEPH'S STORE

1776

21

Sebastian Sheep

Sebastian is a fluffy little sheep who hasn't been shorn yet! During colonial times, young people helped to care for the family's livestock. Sheep, cows, horses, chickens, and ducks had to be tended to. Early in June, the sheep would be washed, and then a couple of days later the sheepshearing would take place. The boys, especially, were involved in this activity. First the sheep had to be herded together, then driven home and placed in a stable. The barn had to be cleaned and the floor swept. As the sheep were shorn, the matted wool would fall on the floor around them. After the fleece was removed, the sheep was so much smaller that it didn't seem like the same animal. Now the sheep could spend a cool, happy summer frolicking in the fields with their new short coat of fur.

Here's what is needed:

7″ square of white oaktag
21 cotton balls, tracing paper
pencil, scissors, white glue
pink and black felt-tip markers

Here's how to do it:

1. Trace the pattern for the sheep on the tracing paper. Put the tracing paper pattern on top of the square of oaktag and hold them together with one hand. With the other hand, cut all around the outside edge of the sheep.

2. Draw in the eye with the black marker. Draw in the nose and the inside of the ear with the pink marker. Repeat this on the other side of the sheep.

3. Glue ten cotton balls onto each side of the sheep. Cover the entire sheep, leaving just enough space for the eyes, nose, and inside of the ears to show through. The remaining cotton ball should be glued on for the sheep's tail.

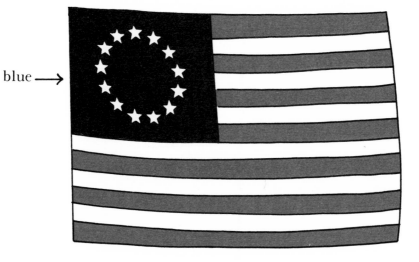

blue →

C Grand Union Flag

← blue

British Union Jack

Colonial Banners

Everyone is familiar with our American flag, "Old Glory," whose stars and stripes have symbolized our country since an act of the Continental Congress on June 14, 1777. Before our independence, however, many different flags flew over our land, from the first Viking banner, the Royal Standard of Spain, the British Union Jack, the flag of the Dutch East India Company, the Royal French Fleur-de-Lis, to the colonial banner of the Revolution.

Today the flag stands as a proud symbol of the people of this country, who united here from many different backgrounds in the pursuit of life, liberty, and happiness.

Wouldn't it be fun to make your very own flag or banner to decorate your room at home or classroom at school? Use some of the old designs: the first United States flag, also known as the Grand Union flag; the Raven flag of the Vikings, which was hoisted by Leif Eriksson around A.D. 1000 during his voyage to America; the Dutch East India flag; the French Fleur-de-Lis flag, which flew over much of what is now the Midwest and Louisiana; and the British Union Jack.

Here's what is needed:

1 yard of muslin
yellow, orange, red, and blue medium-width felt-tip markers
black fine-line felt-tip marker, pencil, ruler
scissors, tape, brown wrapping paper

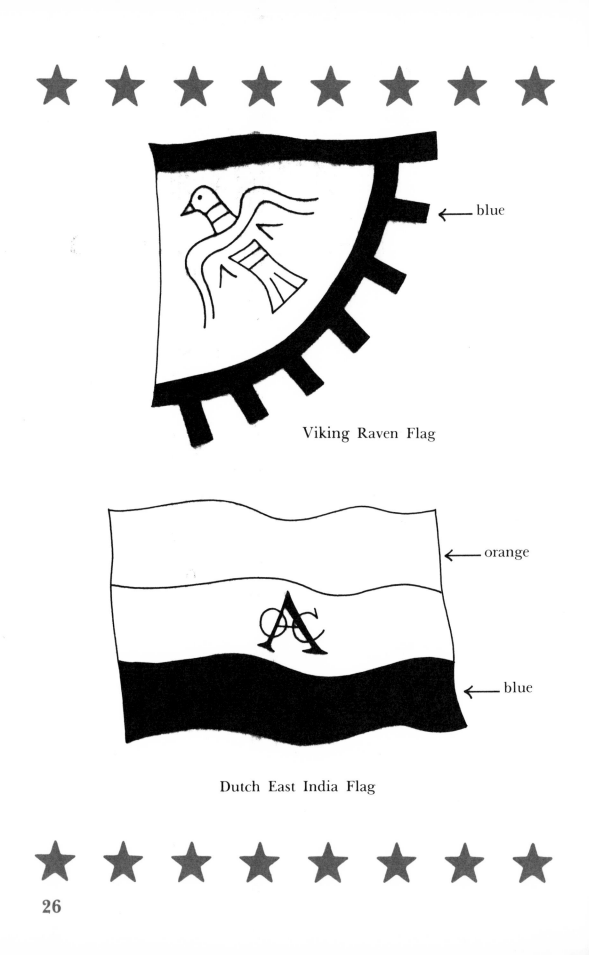

Viking Raven Flag

Dutch East India Flag

Here's how to do it:

1. For each of the banners, you will need to cut the muslin into a rectangle 11 inches by 17 inches. You may need some help with this. Ask an adult to give you a hand.

2. Prepare your work surface by placing a sheet of brown wrapping paper, larger than your piece of muslin, on your work table. Now tape the piece of muslin that is to be your banner to the wrapping paper by placing a small piece of tape on each of the corners. If you have to color in these areas, you can touch them up after you have finished coloring in the rest of your banner.

3. Choose which one of the designs you are going to make and sketch it in lightly on the muslin. You might want to draw the stripes with a ruler.

4. With a black fine-line felt-tip marker, go over the pencil lines. Color in the banner with the markers as shown. Repeat for each of the designs given.

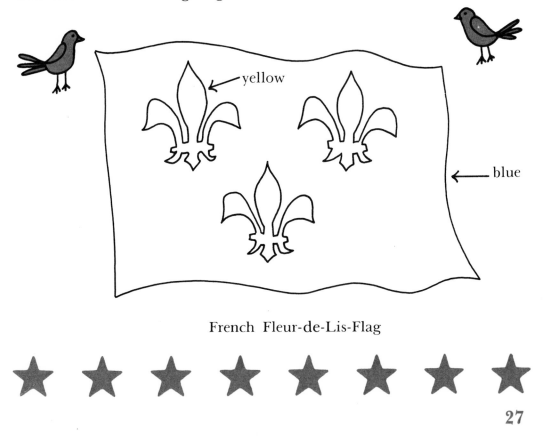

yellow

blue

French Fleur-de-Lis-Flag

Country Diary

★

Start a diary today! Below are directions for making a little book to begin to write your thoughts in. Keep this somewhere safe and write down your feelings, what you did during the day, and stories about your family, friends, and pets. You can even keep track of your friends' birthdays in it and take it along on a vacation.

Children long ago kept diaries. Their plain words and emotions express a lively spirit that questioned the world around them and left valuable firsthand accounts of how they lived.

Here's what is needed:

2 sheets of 8½″ × 11″ white drawing paper (use paper slightly thicker than typing paper so that the drawings won't show through)

8½″ × 11″ piece of yellow construction paper, white glue

black fine-line felt-tip marker, pencil, ruler

Here's how to do it:

1. To make the pages for the mini-book, fold each of the two sheets of white paper in half along the width.

2. Fold the sheet of yellow construction paper in half along the width. This will be the cover for the book. The actual finished size of the book is 5½″ wide by 8½″ high.

3. Open up all the folded pages, including the cover, to begin gluing the book together. Place the open cover sheet face down on the table and carefully spread a thin line of glue all along the center fold. Press the first sheet of white paper down onto the cover, making sure to line up the center folds. Now put a

thin line of glue along the fold of this sheet and press the second sheet down all along the fold. Allow to dry for 15 minutes.

4. When the glue has dried, fold the book back to its 5½″ × 8½″ size, with the front cover facing you. Write your name and the date on it with the black marker. Check the illustration for some ideas on how to decorate the cover and inside pages of your diary.

Weather Lore

In today's world the weather doesn't affect our lives as much as it did in colonial times. In the seventeenth and eighteenth centuries, the work that people were able to accomplish had a lot to do with the weather conditions. Dirt roads flooded easily; there were no indoor greenhouses and no automatic sprinkler systems to water crops. Travelers needed to know when there was a full moon and plenty of light so they could see their way on a night journey. Riverboats, which were the main means of transporting goods to market, needed to know the time and size of the tides.

The colonists kept a record, or diary, of the weather and about daily life to help them plan ahead. These records provided important facts and information, the most famous one being *Poor Richard's Almanack*, written by Benjamin Franklin. It included weather predictions, factual records, and tide, sun, moon, and farming guides. This information that people kept in their diaries was added to year after year so that predictions could be made. You can make and keep your own diary by following the directions given on page 28 or you can make a weather lore picture.

Using some of the weather lore that has survived to this day, it might be fun to make a little picture. The border designs given are easy to copy and the weather lore that you choose to write can be written inside. Check the illustrations for proper placement and ideas for making your weather lore picture.

Here's what is needed:

8½″ × 11″ piece of white paper
¼ cup instant coffee or 3 tea bags
waxed paper, pencil, black fine-line felt-tip marker

Here's how to do it:

1. Fill the kitchen sink with about 2″ of warm water. Add ¼ cup instant coffee or the three tea bags.

2. Carefully place the paper in the sink and soak it. The paper becomes very delicate when it is wet, so try not to move it around too much or it will tear. The paper will wrinkle, which is part of the antique look.

3. Leave the paper in the coffee or tea solution for about three minutes, or until it is a little darker than the color you want. The paper will dry a lighter color than it looks when it is wet.

4. Holding the paper at the corners, lightly and carefully shake off the excess liquid. Place the antiqued paper on a piece of waxed paper and allow it to dry for about a half hour.

5. Draw the design for the border onto the antiqued paper with a pencil. Then go over it with a felt-tip marker. Choose which weather lore you like and write it inside the border.

April showers bring May flowers.

If smoke flies low watch for a blow.

Red sky at night means sailor's delight.

Red sky at morn means sailor's forlorn.

When the dew is on the grass rain will never pass.

When grass is dry at morning light, look for rain before tonight.

Swallows flying way up high mean there's no rain in the sky.

Swallows flying near the ground mean a storm will come around.

A halo around the sun or moon means a lengthy slow rain ahead.

Smoke refusing to rise means an oncoming storm.

Daisy Chains

★

Colonial children collected daisies and other wildflowers from the village green, their yards, or nearby fields. You can either pick your own daisies or buy them in the local fruit and vegetable market or flower shop.

Here's what is needed:

a bunch of daisies
small scissors

Here's how to do it:

1. Pinch off the leaves from the stems of the daisies. Make a small slit in each stem with a scissors or your fingernail, as shown in the illustration.

2. Put the stem of the next flower through the slit and carefully pull it up tight. Continue this until the chain is as long as you want it to be. You can wear the chain on your wrist or around your head or just make long chains.

slit

Humming Toy ★

Young Indians, like their colonial counterparts, had to make their own toys and games. These pastimes or crafts are filled with tradition. Years ago, climate, available materials, the events of daily life—hunting, fishing, growing corn—influenced everything the Indians did. The humming toy and darts are decorated with colors and designs that have special meanings.

Colors

WHITE means clear water, also day.

BLACK means growth and the life cycle from birth to death; a black-and-white feather means completeness.

GRAY is for gloom and fatigue.

BLUE is for the sky; it also means power and long-lasting.

RED stands for morning or evening; it can also mean good health.

YELLOW means a sunny day, and the moon.

ORANGE means the return of calm after a storm, and making peace with a friend or enemy.

The directions of the compass are also represented by colors: red = north, white = south, yellow = east, black = west.

Designs

A circle represents everlasting life as well as goodness.

An arrow pointing up is day, and an arrow pointing down means night.

An arrow pointing down also means no return.

An arrow pointing horizontally means straight ahead.

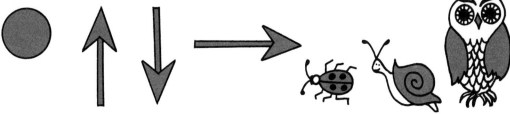

Here's what is needed:

large coat button (about 3″) or a circle of cardboard with two
  holes cut into it, as shown in the illustration
cardboard, scissors, white glue, colored felt-tip markers
36″ piece of heavy string

Here's how to do it:

1. Cut a circle cardboard as shown in the illustration. Color in with the felt-tip markers.

2. Run the string through the holes in the circle (or button) and tie. Turn the circle around and around until the string is tightly wound. Then as you pull the string, the toy will unwind rapidly, making a humming sound.

★ ★ ★ ★ ★ ★ ★ ★ ★

Corn Darts Game

Here's what is needed:

1 dried corn cob (cut into four equal parts). This will give
  you four darts.
small knife (ask an adult for help in using it)
4 2" nails with large heads (one for each dart)
clay, white glue, 12 feathers (3 for each dart)
colored felt-tip markers to decorate the darts, rope

Here's how to do it:

1. First hollow out the centers of each piece of the dried corn
cob.

2. Fill in the hollows with clay. Stick a large nail in the clay,
leaving the point sticking out. Make sure the nail is about
halfway into the cob. Repeat for other darts.

3. Stick three feathers in the top of each dart. Glue to secure
them and allow them to dry.

4. For the target, make a circle of rope about 8" in diameter.
Tie the ends together. To play the game, place the circle on
the ground, outdoors, at a marked distance from the players.
The winner is the one who gets the most darts in the ring.

Note: You will need to be very careful when playing with this
project.

①

②

③

④

Eli and Sara

These pleasant little dolls are easy to make by just folding and tying corn husks together.

Here's what is needed:

dried corn husks (The outside leaves of the corn that have been pulled away from the corn cob and allowed to dry out. Husks from one ear of corn will make one doll.)
bowl of warm water
scissors, string, black felt-tip marker
scraps of fabric for clothing

Here's how to do it:

1. Soak the corn husks in the warm water to make them easier to work with.

2. Fold several large husks in half and tie a piece of string near the fold to make the head.

3. Underneath the string, insert two or three smaller husks for arms. Now tie another string below the arms.

4. Shape the bottom half of the doll into legs, tying each ankle with string. You can make your doll some clothes with the scraps of fabric. It might be fun to make two dolls—a boy and a girl. Check the illustration for ideas.

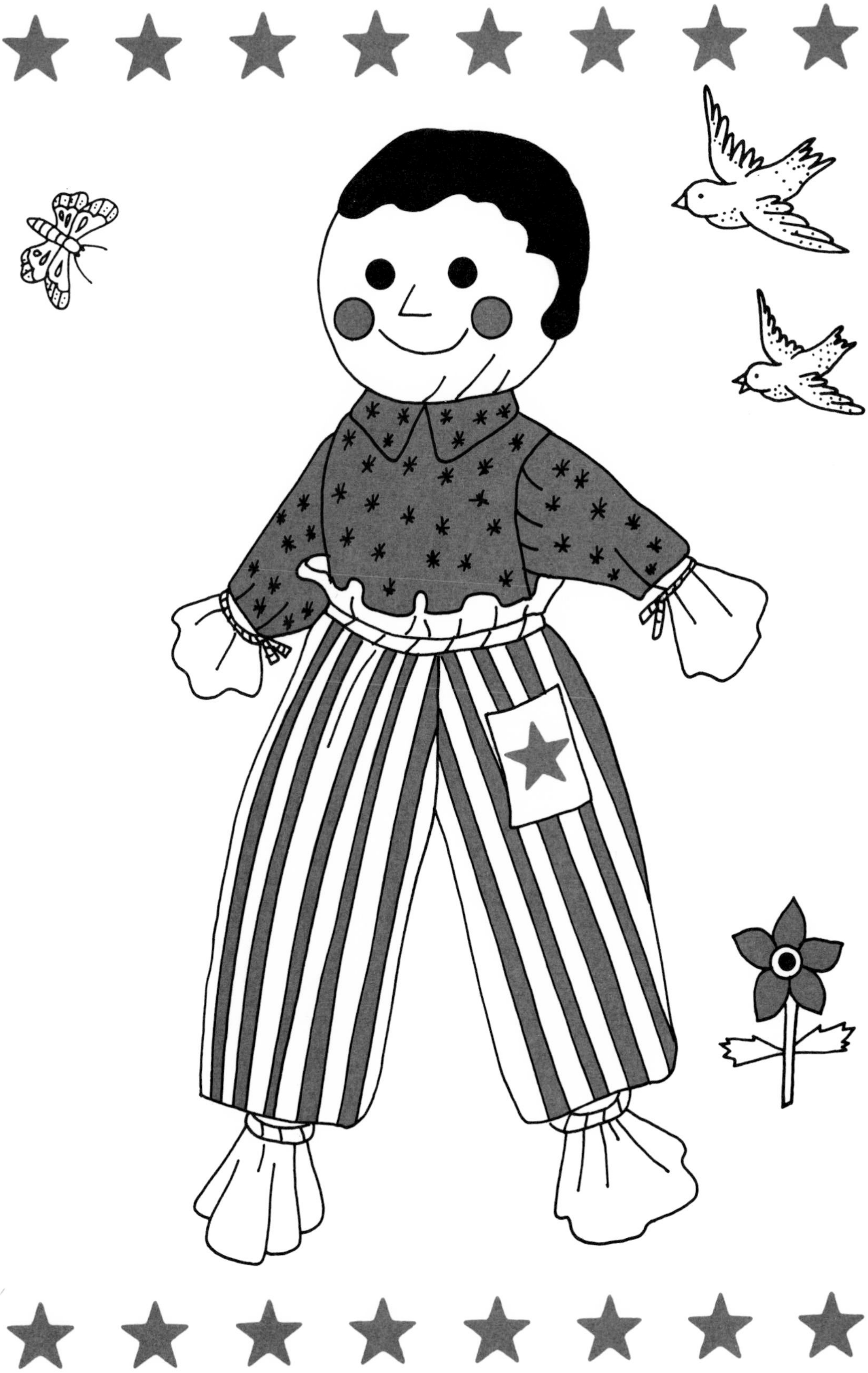

Pressed Flowers

Pressed flowers keep their color beautifully and can be saved forever. Try pressing buttercups, daisies, black-eyed Susans, or any of your favorite flowers.

Here's what is needed:

flowers
2 pieces of paper towel
4 heavy books
8½″ × 11″ piece of white paper, glue, 8″ piece of ribbon

Here's how to do it:

1. While the flowers are still fresh and flexible, spread them on one piece of paper towel. Place the other paper towel on top.

2. Gently put the flowers on a clean surface where they won't be disturbed. A corner of your desk would be a good place to do this. Place the books on top of the paper towel. Leave for three to four days.

3. Carefully remove the books from the paper towels.

4. Make a nice arrangement of your dried flowers on the sheet of white paper. Handle the dried flowers carefully. Don't worry if some of the petals fall off. Gently glue down your bouquet. Tie the ribbon into a bow. Glue the bow onto the paper.

Pomander Balls

Fragrant pomander balls were used by colonial women to hide unpleasant household smells. They were tucked into cupboards, drawers, and baskets so that their sweet, spicy scent could be enjoyed. Several could be put into a fancy bowl and placed on a table for a special occasion.

Here's what is needed:

firm, ripe oranges, lemons, or limes
jar of whole cloves
toothpick, dish of powdered cinnamon
pieces of fancy ribbon, string, scissors

Here's how to do it:

1. With the toothpick, make tiny holes in the skin of the fruit. Keep the holes close together. Gently push a whole clove into each hole. Cover the entire surface of the fruit with cloves.

2. Roll the fruit in the cinnamon. Put the fruit on a dish and place it in a cool, dark, dry place for two to three weeks. A closet is a good place to do this. After the fruit has dried out, it will shrink a little. It should smell wonderful. You can tie a piece of fancy ribbon around each ball to decorate it.

Indian Pudding ★

This Indian Pudding is an authentic American treat. It was a special dessert that was served during colonial times. It was baked in a slow oven. Today it can be enjoyed either plain or with vanilla ice cream.

Ingredients:

¼ cup sugar
2 teaspoons cinnamon
1 teaspoon salt
½ cup light molasses
3 eggs, beaten
⅓ cup yellow cornmeal
3½ cups milk
1 tablespoon butter
½ cup seedless raisins
extra butter to grease the
  baking pan
vanilla ice cream

Utensils:

large mixing bowl
mixing spoon
measuring cups and spoons
small saucepan
8″ × 8″ × 2″ baking dish
toothpick

Here's how to do it:

1. Preheat the oven to 325°. Ask an adult to help you with this. In the large bowl, combine the sugar, cinnamon, salt, molasses, and eggs. Stir until it is smooth.

2. In the small saucepan, combine the cornmeal and milk. Cook over low heat for about 10 minutes, stirring constantly.

3. Remove the saucepan from the heat and add the butter. Add to the molasses mixture in the large bowl and stir until combined. Add the raisins.

4. Grease the baking dish and then pour the batter into it. Bake the pudding for 50 minutes, or until a toothpick inserted into the center comes out clean. Serve warm with vanilla ice cream. Serves six.

Ginger Snaps

These tasty little cookies are a famous old-time treat and won't last long around your house.

Ingredients:	Utensils:
2 cups sifted all-purpose flour	large mixing bowl
3 teaspoons ground ginger	mixing spoon, 2 cookie sheets
1 teaspoon ground cinnamon	measuring cups and spoons
2 teaspoons baking soda	glass
½ teaspoon salt	
¾ cup butter, softened	
1 cup sugar	
1 egg, beaten	
¼ cup molasses	
sugar (for coating, on dinner plate)	

Here's how to do it:

1. Preheat the oven to 350°. Ask an adult to help you with this. Combine the flour, ginger, cinnamon, baking soda, and salt on a large sheet of waxed paper.

2. In the large mixing bowl, beat the butter and sugar until they are creamy. Add the egg and molasses. Stir in the flour mixture until the batter is well blended.

3. Now wash and dry your hands because you are going to be rolling the dough into balls about the size of large marbles. Roll each ball in the sugar that is on the dinner plate until each one is coated with sugar. Place the balls on the cookie sheets about two inches apart and flatten each with the bottom of the glass. Bake the cookies for about 10 to 12 minutes, or until the tops are cracked. Makes about four dozen cookies.

Cranberry Muffins

Spring in the forest provided the colonists with an assortment of wild berries—huckleberries, whortleberries, cranberries, gooseberries, raspberries, elderberries, mulberries, and strawberries. The freshly picked fruits were eaten as they are today, plain, with cream and sugar, or in baked goods. The cranberry is native to America. Early settlers named these plants bearberries, because eastern bears loved to eat them.

The settlers found that the fresh fruit season was short, and so most berries were sugared or otherwise preserved. Berries were dried, pounded into a hard paste, and then cut into squares to be chewed like candy. The fruits were boiled with syrup or sugar to make marmalades and jellies. They were also made into breads, muffins, and little cakes. Berries were also used to make ink and to dye yarn and fabric.

Ingredients:	Utensils:
2 cups sifted all-purpose flour	large mixing bowl
¼ cup sugar	mixing spoon
3 teaspoons baking powder	measuring cups and spoons
½ teaspoon salt	paper baking muffin cups
1 egg, beaten	muffin tins
1 cup milk	
¼ cup butter, melted and cooled	
1 cup freshly washed cranberries	

Here's how to do it:

1. Preheat the oven to 350°. Ask an adult to help you do this. Combine the flour, sugar, baking powder, and salt in the large mixing bowl. Stir until completely combined.

2. Add the egg, milk, and butter. Stir only enough to moisten the dry ingredients. Now add the cranberries.

3. Put the paper baking muffin cups into the muffin tins. Fill each paper cup two-thirds full of batter. Bake for about 20 to 25 minutes or until lightly browned on top. Makes about 10 to 12 muffins.

Candied Orange Peel ★

This was an Elizabethan treat that was brought to America by the colonists. It can be enjoyed today as candy or used in cakes like the Christmas Fruit Cake in the colonial *Home* book on page 46.

Ingredients:

Utensils:

4 oranges
water
sugar

knife
saucepan
bowl
slotted spoon
waxed paper, air-tight container for storage

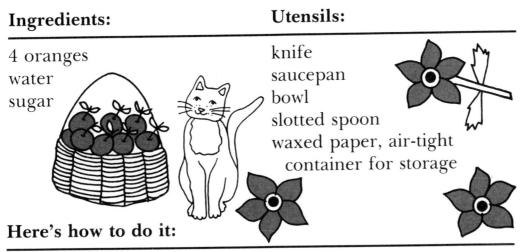

Here's how to do it:

1. Wash the oranges. Quarter the fruit and remove the pulp.

2. Put the peel in a saucepan with enough water to cover it. Bring to a boil and then simmer for 10 minutes.

3. Drain, keeping the liquid in a bowl. Allow peel to cool. Now cut the peel into small strips.

4. Put the liquid in the saucepan, measuring it as you pour it. For each cup of liquid, add 2 cups of sugar. Stir the mixture until combined. Boil for 5 minutes. Add the peel and cook until it is tender and you can almost see through it. There won't be much liquid left and it will be sticky.

5. Using the slotted spoon, remove the peel from the liquid and spread it on the waxed paper. Allow the peel to dry completely. Store in an airtight container. Although the colonists didn't have chocolate, for variety, you can dip the candied orange peel in melted dark chocolate.

Index